Hipnosis

Lost Hip Hop Writings

Cameron Peck

India | USA | UK

Made with ❤ on the BookLeaf Publishing Platform
www.bookleafpub.in
www.bookleafpub.com

Dedication

I'd like to dedicate this book
to the 1's dedicated to books.

Your discography is promising, I promise.

Keep working.

Keep tweaking... the bits and pieces.

The puzzle will be completed... one day.

Preface

in many ways, a book is like a Hip Hop album.

in many ways, an author is like an emcee.

in many ways, you can get from a to b.

that's a line.

Acknowledgements

I'd like to thank BookLeaf Publishing
for creating this opportunity.

I'd like to thank my parents for creating me.

I'd like to thank myself for creating this collection.

1. The Intro

Give my friends reparations
so we can focus on the unity.
I'm at the intersection
of preparation and opportunity.
But I won't call it luck, like the Roman philosopher.
I walked the Earth's surface,
in search of purpose.
I'm a roamin' philosopher.

Give my friends reparations.
Let's focus on the unity.
I'm at the intersection
of preparation and opportunity.
And I'm patiently waiting
to carry my cross across the crosswalk.
Got God all in my headphones. BossTalk.

Give my friends reparations.
Focus on the energy.
I'm at the intersection
of preparation and opportunity.
And I'm not crashin' out.
When the pressure's on, I'm cashing' out.

2. Track Two 2

Contract maxed out...

I'm playing for the Gods.

they signed a Demon to get even.

How odd.

I'm seasoned.

3. The Vice

I'm a Godly novice.

It's odd I got no audience.

Still audible with all da bull.

Still want an audiobook on Audible.

The audacity.

4. Here, for your information.

I'm destined for greatness
in this age of information.
I've been putting information in formation for ages.

The precise placement
of this guys statements
could decide the state of our nation.

Don't get it mistaken.

Even my misses get taken,

and curated into greatness.

5. The Pen

Wicked with the pen
A wizard in the pen

Locked in my mind
Doing my time

Thank God for magic
For getting me out
In the form of ink

From the pen to the page,
I'm freed on this day

6. The Leader

I lead the way with the lead.
I may have led a stray astray.
My lead pencil can be like lead to the mental.
Perhaps it's something we shouldn't get into,
but I'm into it if you are.

I could make you sink, with the ink.

I'm a freak when I leak... on the page.

With the pen, I'm a mage.
I could make your head... change.

I ball with the ball point.
I write joints that spike points.

Im anointed.
Appointed... to voice them.

Divinely elected to express my mere reflections.

7. The Sun

Can't I do it just for fun?

Can't I do it without thinking I'm the one?

But that's part of the fun.

Knowing I'm the Sun.
And the shadows...

Knowing innocence.
And the gallows.

8. Cell

I'm an intelligent movement student,
writing to you from the cell.

I've got a couple questions,
coupled with questionable mental health.

They try to lock us up,
but they don't know the level of intell...

Contained in every cell.

There's an eye that sees,
contained in EVERY cell.

9. WAR

I'm in a warzone.
but I'm not in my war zone.

bunch of warriors brawling.
and I'm taking the high road every time.

it's a battlefield.
but he never feeled like battling.

bunch of demons at each others necks.
I'm next.

10. Crowd

I don't follow the crowd.
That route gets crowded.

I rap to present the gifts I'm endowed with.

I'm high on a mountain.
Don't act unimpressed.

You're high key like Nike.
You "Just Do It" for a check.

But I ain't mad.
Cause I got a logo too.

11. The Wave

a new wave will pave the way very soon.
the moon will set the tide.
the tie dye will splash.

Titans will not clash,
but instead tighten their ties,
and invest in each other.

this is happening in real time.
this wave is the future.
a gift from the Gods.

12. You

Imagine how immaculate you are.

and tactfully intact, with tactics.

It's magic.

Tragically,
you haven't seen
your majesty.

It's simple math to me.

You're an aggregate of all experience.
The entire Universe, in One.

You're the sole solution to mass confusion.

13. Community

I used to be so excited
Thinking I was the first
To do it like me

Then I learned of others
Who did it similar

I was not upset
That I wouldn't be the first

But rather thrilled
That I wasn't alone

With that, came strength
And a sense of community

And the best part
I was still doin me

14. Writers' Block

The Mind Set
the gang that bangs
harder than slang

It's like a team of humans,
behind the scenes,
rewriting the code of the Universe.

reshaping the mentality of the whole humanity

those of us
that innovate with a pen

those of us
that inspire readers across the world
to think new things
and writers across the world
to be original

we may not get the shine of mainstream celebrities
but our light is bright for all to see
it shines through everyone
we pave the way
with courage, vulnerability, and God-given ability

15. PRO

My approach
to becoming a pro
is appropriate.

a pro of me becoming a pro is that i'm approaching a
progressive program update for all to download

download this update real quick:

"My approach to becoming a pro is appropriate."

16. My First Love Poem

Here I sit

You're thousands of miles away

I have no idea what you're doing

and why you're doing it over there

I have no idea what im doing

and why im doing it over here

I'm thousands of miles away

Yet here I sit

I must be stupid

17. The Senses

You satisfy every one of my senses

Therefore, I won't be sad if i
spend every one of my cents on you

the scent on you is now left on me

rightfully so

when im with you,
I cant afford to be anything but free

I do what I please
and somehow, it always pleases you

you invest in me
and I return the favor

that's compound interest

we requested ecstasy
next thing I know,
you're laying next to me

18. IF ONLY

I try to hold her close
She just turns her back

I want her to wake up
and trade me love for love

Maybe someday...

19. The Hurt

I hurt you, unintentionally

You struck back with a vicious vengeance

a switch had been flipped

I was instantly your enemy, feeling your wrath

I could see you were not hating me,
but loving yourself

so I loved it

I stand behind you

even when it seems im standing in your way

20. Lottery Ticket

I don't think anyone has noticed,
But my potion is potent
But I'm losing focus

I wouldn't be broke if,
More people were paying attention

To be broke is to be neglected
Not receiving affection

Currently earning currency
On the daily

Been working on myself a lot
Pay me

Tired of trading time for money
Especially at the going rate

Cashing in this lottery ticket
I've got the winning numbers

21. Justin Case

Just in case this is goodbye

And a 2nd book i never write

I hope you had a good time

And remember why
You do what you do